People, Plannin Video Gam

Supplemental Game Production Guide

By Gerard C. Merritt, MBA, CSM, CSP

Edited by Rochelle Spencer, MFA

CelleC Games™ Publishing

CelleC Games ™ Publishing
Orlando, FL 32810
Publishing@CelleCGames.com

Edited by Rochelle Spencer

Copy edited by Ed Younskevicius

Printed in the United States of America

Publisher's Cataloging-in-Publication Data

Merritt, Gerard C.
    People, planning, and production for video game development : supplemental game production guide / by Gerard C. Merritt, MBA, CSM, CSP ; edited by Rochelle Spencer, MFA.
      p. cm.
    ISBN: 978-0-985501-20-4

    1. Video games—Design. 2. Computer games—Design. 3. Computer games—Programming. I. Spencer, Rochelle, ed. II. Title.
QA76.76.C672 M47 2011
794.8—dc22

                                   2010942273

About the Author

Gerard C. Merritt, MBA, CSM, CSP has over fifteen years of experience with technology, project management, business operations management, and the Software Development Life Cycle. His professional experience has frequently combined technical knowledge with business operations to successfully develop and integrate technologies supporting broad–ranging organizational needs. He has a Bachelor of Science in Electrical Engineering Technologies from the University of Central Florida and a Master of Business Administration in Marketing with a specialization in Operations from the Crummer School of Business at Rollins College. He has also worked for companies such as Siemens Telecom Networks, Lockheed Martin, Electronic Arts, Law & Associates, Connextions, and Full Sail University. While at Lockheed Martin, he graduated from their Operations Leadership Development Program (OLDP), acquired the Scrum Master and Scrum Professional certifications, and achieved a Green Belt in Lean Six Sigma. Gerard continues to develop himself professionally by relentlessly exploring newer and more sophisticated technology and recognizing that agile methodology knowledge is pivotal to his growth.

Acknowledgements

I would like to thank my dear family and friends who supported and pushed me through this. Also I would like to thank my colleagues and students for their myriad of questions that evoked my many notes that are now forever bound in this book…

Table of Contents

Objectives from Reading and Understanding this Guidebook

General

- **Consistent Processes.** Establish a consistent set of game management tools and processes that can be used across many game development projects.

People

- **Productive Assessment.** Understand resources' capabilities to aid in a defined game development life cycle. Working toward the team's strengths while stretching them is key and essential for growth.

- **Healthy Relationship Management.** Building trust and maintaining respect throughout the game development life cycle is vital to overall team health, which directly impacts game quality.

- **Consistent Communication.** Establish a consistent process that can be used across all teams for communicating information on a regular basis. Essentially, this means game producers serve as a liaison, mediator, and communicator between all parties.

Planning

- **Organic Documentation.** Plans are not written in concrete and can expand and contract through production. Allow for flexibility and always maintain your original documentation.

- **Solid Preproduction.** Author and ensure solid project planning. This also includes identifying critical features and tasks that need thorough review, which sometimes get missed in the hectic schedule.

- **Continuous Project Analysis and Risk Tracking.** Maintain accurate status reporting throughout. Identify and communicate risks to all parties to encourage absolute involvement.

- **Game Production Merged with Game Design.** With poor workflow tracking, game production can easily diverge from the initial game design and requirements. The production goal is to maintain game development through continual tracking, review, and communication.

- **Acquiring All Prerequisites.** Have the access, licensees, hardware, and training required to successfully start production.

Production

- **On-time Scheduling.** To maintain a good workflow, establish consistent processes for tracking progress on an ongoing basis. Utilize planning tools to aid in game project maintenance where applicable. Have an affinity for delivering on or before deadline.

- **Establishing a Quality Philosophy, and Quality Assessment.** Establish high quality expectations that are consistent throughout the entire team.

- **Functional, Tangible Deliverables**. Milestone deliverables should have detailed completion criteria. This will require the team to clearly identify game functionality for each milestone and track their progress towards reaching those goals.

- **Accurate Budgeting.** Consider determining and tracking the overall budget and schedule for game production. Work with leads to track the completion of individual steps.

Producer / Production Leader: Know Your Role

Understanding Your Role

Producer – Production Leader – Game Project Manager

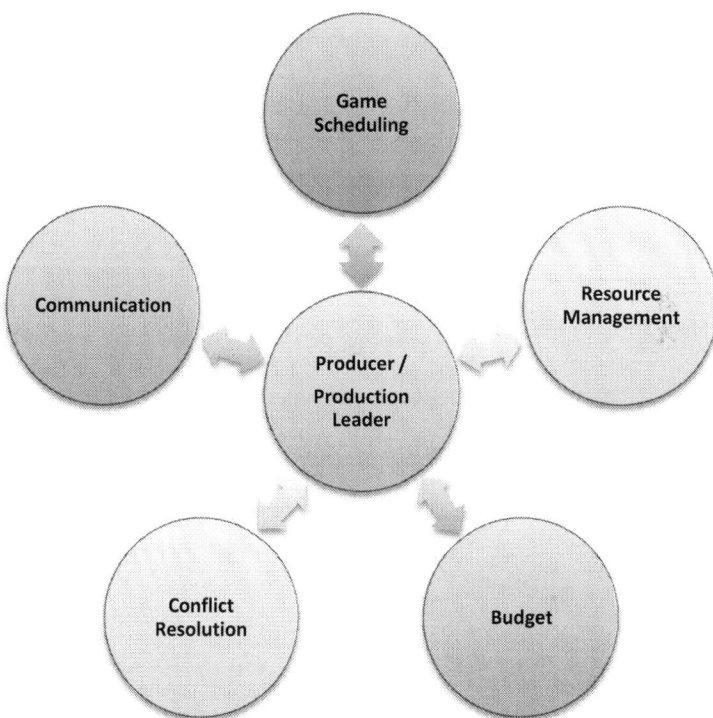

First and foremost the person orchestrating and managing the game production must understand the role and all the positives and negatives that come with being a manager. These responsibilities include the following:

- **Scheduling.** Maintain all planning documentation and never abandon the project documentation under pressure. Record and analyze all modifications to the schedule, and always conduct contingency planning throughout.

- **Communication.** Discuss the status of the project on a daily basis with leads, and on a weekly basis with the team and stakeholders.

- **Providing a Single Point of Contact.** Provide a single point of contact for the game project for all stakeholders. Build effective relationships with all team members and stakeholders.
- **Oversight.** Oversee all game development aspects, including schedules, quality, risk analysis, and adherence to required processes.

- **Estimation.** Review overall estimates regularly for consistency and identify anything abnormal. Also compare estimated production costs versus actual production costs.

- **Status Reporting.** Establish a consistent project report process. Identify what data/metrics should be tracked and reported and work with team leads to provide this. Consolidate all project statuses into one source.

- **Tracking Production.** Manage/track game production tasks.

- **Risk Assessment.** Identify risks and issues and ensure their resolution.

- **Conducting Milestone Reviews.** Conduct milestone reviews for all projects.

- **Risk Prioritization.** Ensure high-risk items are flagged early and tracked through till decision date.

- **Risk Assessment.** Continually assess risks.

- **Problem Solving.** Facilitate problem solving, as well as conflict resolution. Determine resources needed to resolve issues and utilize these resources when necessary.

- **Quality Assurance.** Establish a quality philosophy in the preproduction phase and discuss this philosophy with your staff. Maintain a consistent philosophy throughout all phases of production.

- **Tracking Metrics.** Establish game quality metrics that will be tracked. This may include:
o Feature Completion Rate
o Estimated Time vs. Actual Time
o Bug Count vs. Bug Close

The Five Key Pillars: Know Who & What Is Important

The Five Pillars

As a producer / game production leader, you should recognize five key pillars that have to be balanced throughout the game development life cycle. They are: Team, Game, Client, Internal Stakeholders, and Documentation. Each pillar is different even though some may share commonalities.

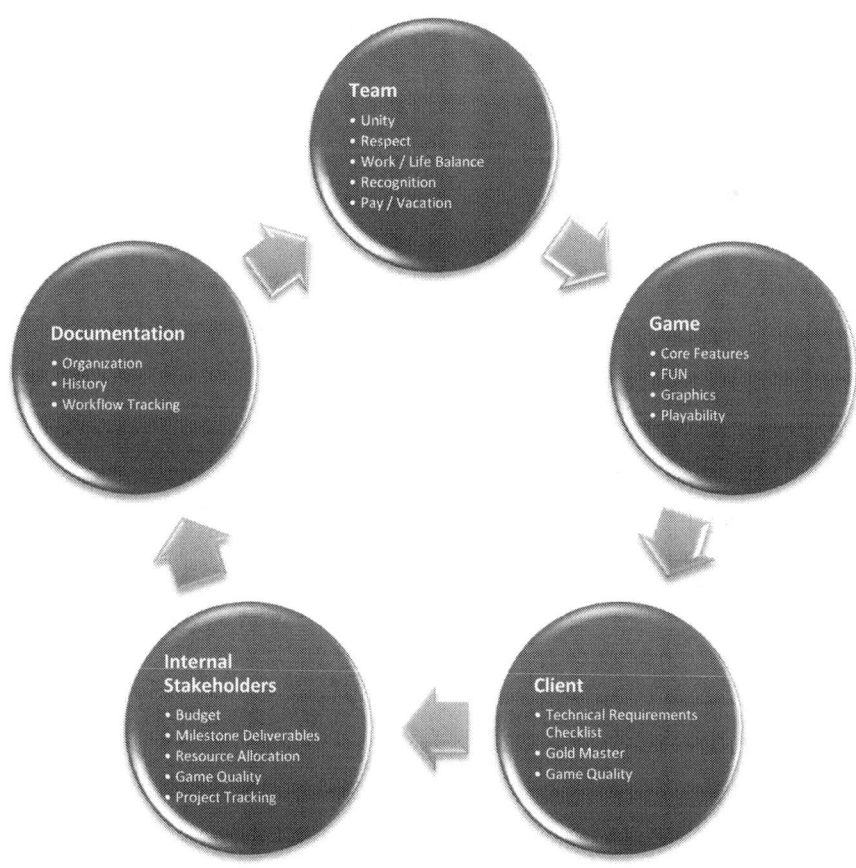

Team Pillar

There is no particular hierarchy to team-building; each element is as important as every other. In the game development life cycle they all play integral roles with each other. Key aspects of this pillar are:

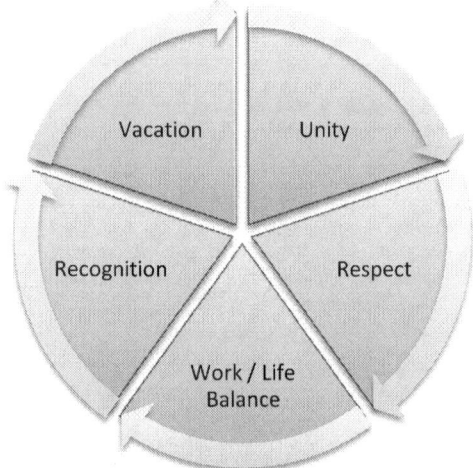

- **Unity** – The unity of a team is crucial to the successful development of a high-quality game. Dysfunction can not only wreak havoc on the people that embody the team, but can also jeopardize the overall quality level of the game itself. Team unity is not just a "touchy-feely" thing but is, in fact, an essential ingredient for the mental health of the group. It is something that cannot be measured or calculated but must be present and sustained throughout.

- **Respect** – Acknowledgment of people's dedication and quality work is vital to the team's health and adds value to the unity factor.

- **Work / Life Balance** – People are the heart of the game-making process, and without them, the game could not be developed. By incorporating flexibility, balance, and freedom into the team's work schedule, the production leader grants the opportunity for team members to recharge and refocus.

- **Recognition** – This is the simple human part of being a good leader. Be able to praise the person or persons who put forth good effort resulting in quality work.

- **Vacation** – Vacation should be used as a reward for those who not only work hard, but also provide issue-free code and/or art. This is work that adds significant value by allowing the team to meet scheduled deadlines or even to complete work well ahead of time.

Game Pillar

Unlike the team pillar, certain factors under the game pillar are higher-ranked or weighted more than others. The game's success ultimately depends upon prioritization and what principles are most important to your team, organization, and/or company. Key aspects of this pillar are:

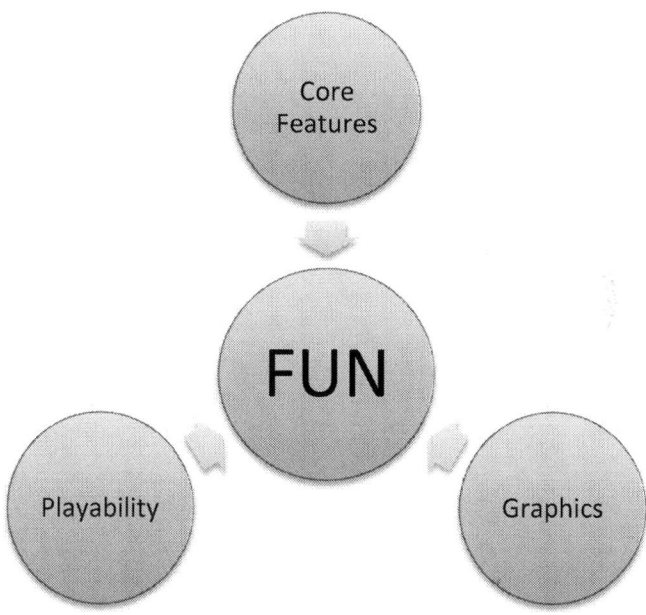

- **Core Features** – The core features of a game determine its genre and capabilities. These features are also the foundation for the fun.

- **Fun** – This is the intangible factor that can "make" a game the next AAA title and earn it the title of "This Year's Blockbuster," or "break" a game and plunge it in the $5.00 bin in the local game store. Fun is needed to make the game sellable, memorable, and replayable. FUN is based upon Core Features, Graphics, and Playability.

- **Graphics** – Video games are a visual medium. Graphics support the code as actors support a screenplay.

- **Playability** – Game function is another part of what makes games fun. If the game does not function, i.e., play the way that is required, then the player will be adversely affected.

Client Pillar

Clients and manufacturers all want the best games for their respective consoles. In a perfect world, "Triple A" status for the majority of games would be ideal. However, clients and manufacturers do not control that aspect. Instead, they each have their own benchmark standards that developers must meet to make commercial games. Key aspects of this pillar are:

- **Technical Requirements Checklist (TRC)** – The manufacturers' stringent guidelines for the game to operate on their consoles. A common example: if a controller becomes disconnected from the console for any reason, the game must pause unless in online gameplay.

- **Game Quality** – Manufacturers want high quality for the prospective title that will be a part of their game libraries. The game must pass all TRCs and must also have all the features that were submitted with the game proposal from the developer.

- **Gold Master** – Signifies that the game has passed both the developer's and manufacturers' criteria and is ready for mass duplication. This only occurs after successful TRC submission.

Internal Stakeholders Pillar

Internal stakeholders are the executive leaders of the company that care about the bottom line and overall welfare of the company. They should be strategic in thinking and methodical in execution of any plan. The key line items on the radar for these people include, but are not limited to, the following:

- **Budget** – The financial aspect of projects. Internal stakeholders are highly conscious of the company's profit and loss margins, and success is measured by how much profits increase (or decrease).

- **Milestone Deliverables** – Some studios have their budgets based on milestone payments that correlate to milestone deliverables. Therefore, this can be an important factor in deciding what has to get completed next for the game project.

- **Game Quality** – Each game studio has its own game quality tenets. Some focus specifically on visuals and let game functionality follow, while others have high functionality and decent graphics as their measures of quality instead.

- **Resource Allocation** – Internal stakeholders are aware of the company's intellectual property, i.e. they are subject matter experts (SMEs). It would be ideal if there were SMEs on every team, but this may not always be possible. For game projects that are of great importance, the internal stakeholders will make sure SME resources spend the most time with them.

- **Project Tracking** – This is the overall management of the game project. Managing deadlines, budgets, and expectations can be quite a task in and of itself. However, the internal stakeholders are primarily focused on keeping the project on time and under budget.

Documentation Pillar

Documentation is the focal point of preproduction and production. The documentation becomes the team's roadmap, leading them from point of origin to the game's completion. Through the journey of production, avoiding issues and (sometimes) changing course are both critical points for the success of the project. Once again, documentation is a roadmap, not an unchangeable manuscript locked in concrete. Documentation is an organic, living, and ever-changing source of information. Key aspects of this pillar are:

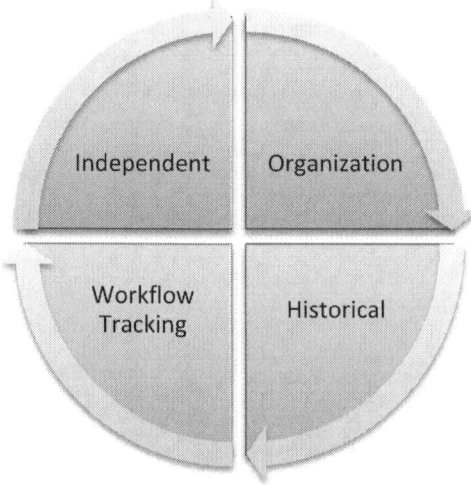

- **Organization** – Documentation needs to be organized, from folder location on the network all the way down to proper names of files with dates. The time and date stamp on the file can change when it is saved or even just opened, so it is essential to double-check records for accuracy.

- **History** – The historical perspective comes into account after production has begun. Once a milestone has occurred, it generates information and allows synthesis of that information to take place. Understanding the history of your game's development gives you the opportunity to modify estimates and re-evaluate the present and next milestones.

- **Workflow** – The progression of the game development life cycle is crucial to successful game completion. Monitoring tasks to reorganize priorities is vital to the health of production. Remember, the documentation is organic: some parts grow, while others get reduced.

- **Independence** – Documentation needs to be independent of the author. By itself, it should be able to answer any and all questions that may arise.

The Game Development Life Cycle: Knowing the Process

Game development is broken into three phases. Each phase is dependent on the previous phase, and each phase has significant differences. The first phase is preproduction, the second is production, and the third phase is postproduction.

- **Preproduction** – This phase can be considered the planning and roadmap-building phase. It's important in this phase for the producer/production leader to have an understanding of organic documentation; plans are not written in concrete and can expand and contract through production. This also includes identifying critical features and tasks that need thorough review, which sometimes get missed in the hectic schedule.

Goals for Preproduction
1. Complete all necessary documentation
2. Verify estimates
3. Review with stakeholders
4. Have kickoff meeting with team to set expectations

- **Production** – AKA "when the tires hit the road." This is where the producer / production leader has to take all the documentation that was developed and actually use it in production. The producer also has to ensure game production does not diverge from the game design. With poor workflow tracking, game production can easily deviate from the initial game design and requirements. The goal of production is to keep game development moving through continual tracking, review, and communication.

Goals for Production
1. Meet milestone deliverables
2. Manage hours
3. Keep team motivated
4. Stay within or below budget
5. Track workflow properly
6. Keep stakeholders informed
7. Keep communication flowing throughout the team
8. Be transparent with the team
9. Manage all forms of change, from resources to features
10. Manage conflicts
11. Maintain the highest game quality possible
12. Keep bug count low while fixing "A" & "B" priority bugs immediately

9

- **Postproduction** – Game production closes out. In other words, the postproduction phase is the final phase in which all game project items are closed. The producer has to be mindful of all the acceptance criteria for the project in this phase, which may be studio-specific as well as client-specific. Archiving, one of the general activities of postproduction, will also be done in this phase and monitored until completion. Finally, the post-mortem presentation is an opportunity for the producer and some members of the team to discuss the things that went right, the things that went wrong, and how production went overall.

Goals for Postproduction

1. Produce gold master
2. Conduct game post-mortem
3. Finish game archive
4. Have game wrap party
5. Conduct game closeout meeting

Assessing the Resources: Know Your Team

Assessing the Resources

Prior to starting any game development, it is imperative that an assessment of the resources is done. This is a simple process that can be done in two steps. First, an initial interview with each team member will aid you in understanding their specific niche and their level of expertise, as well as finding out what they would like to contribute to the overall game. Second, developing a skills matrix of all the resources and skill sets that are present will allow you to assess individuals in the organization as potential team members.

TEAM: Bottle Top Rockets

	Lua		C#		C++		AI		Networking		Gameplay		Adobe PS		3Ds Max		Maya	
		LOE		LOE		LOE		LOE		LOE		LOE		LOE		LOE		LOE
Development Team																		
Christian Warrick		S	X	S	X	M	X	M			X	S						
Larry Hughes							X	M			X	S						
Tom Jenkins							X	S	X	S								
Lisa Rey					X	S	X	S	X	M								
Isaiah West											X	J						
Tony Williams		J	X	J	X	S	X	S	X	J								
Art Team																		
Rick James							X	S					X	S	X	S	X	S
Debbie Reins							X	S					X	S	X	M	X	J
Kerry Jordan													X	S	X	M	X	J
Howard Mills							X	M					X	M	X	M		
Jade Blake							X	J					X	J	X	J	X	M
Gilmore Homes							X	J					X	J	X	J	X	J

LOE – Level of Experience
- S – Senior, having experience that allows them to be considered a subject matter expert
- M – Middle, having credible experience in the subject matter to be able to solve minor to moderately difficult issues.
- J – Junior, having basic knowledge of the subject matter.

The categories presented are not all-encompassing; game development is not limited to only what is shown here. In fact, this is just a small representation of what a real skills matrix would look like. By gaining detailed knowledge of the team's skill sets and expertise, the producer/production leader can make proper judgment calls to mitigate risk on realigned tasks, and also pair program, reassign tasks where necessary, and address bugs.

The benefits of completing this process are:
- Genre decision
- Focused game development
- Individual team members' contributions to the game
- Team unity
- Development plans for individuals

The Circle of Documentation: Game Production Documentation

Circle of Documentation

Document correlation is key to the "Circle of Documentation", a process of correlating independent documents by the data held in each. In the game industry, a producer can be inserted into the production process at any time, and the producer's responsibility–to either develop or maintain current documentation–is essential to completing the game.

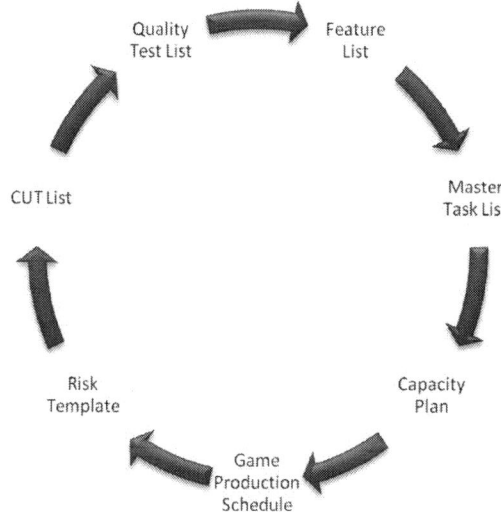

The "Circle of Documentation" consists of but is not limited to the following:

- Feature List
- Master Task List
- Capacity Plan
- Game Production Schedule
- Risk Template
- Cut List
- Quality Test List

The reason this list is not set in stone is the same reason why the game industry is relegated to the entertainment sector and is not considered true technology: lack of standardization. Even now, some may read this handbook and fully support the ideas explored within it, while others may feel less comfortable working in an industry that is so dynamic and individualized. This is the challenge—and the benefit—of working in the game industry: it offers opportunity for discovery and innovation in a constantly evolving and immensely creative field.

Feature List: Game Features

The feature list is a list of all features to be realized in the game. This also includes tools that will be utilized in developing the game and the systems in the background that support gameplay feature functionality.

			Cryptic Corners (Fighter) Features List Legend: Priority/Difficulty: 1 = Highest, 3 = Lowest			
Code	Type	Category	Feature	Priority	Difficulty	Milesto
GP1.1.0	Core	System	**Game engine** supporting game physics, lighting, algorithms	1	1	1
GP1.2.0	Core	Gameplay	**Playable characters** that a player can select in-game and utilize in game combat	1	1	1
GP1.3.0	Core	System	**Opponent AI system** supporting computer-controlled attack, defense, and combo systems	1	1	1
GP1.4.0	Core	System	**Collision system** supporting all weapons, particle effects, characters, and stage floor	1	1	1
GP1.5.0	Core	System	**Particle effect system** supporting weapon, special move, and physical damage attacks	1	1	1
PD1.1.0	Core	Tools	**Maya** will be used to create all art assets for the game project	1	1	1
PD1.2.0	Core	Tools	**C++** will be used to create all the code for the game project	1	1	1
PD1.3.0	Core	Tools	**Visual Studio 2008** will be used for all debugging during the game project	2	2	1
PD1.4.0	Core	Tools	**MS Project** will be used to coordinate all scheduling, resources, and tasks for the game project	2	3	1
PD1.5.0	Core	Tools	**Lua scripting** will be used to efficiently change values, assets, and gameplay following quality testing	3	2	1
PC1.1.0	Core	Process	**Pair programming** will be utilized to ensure code quality and the coding standard	1	1	1
PC1.2.0	Core	Process	**Risk analysis** will utilized to identify potential risks early and activate planned responses if a risk trigger occurs	1	2	1
PC1.3.0	Core	Process	**Quality testing** will be performed to ensure deliverables meet established criteria for the game project	1	2	1
PC1.4.0	Core	Process	**Turbo Team Meetings** will be held every workday to update the project team on tasks, resources, risks, and the schedule	1	3	1
PC1.5.0	Core	Process	**Rules of conduct** will be established and enforced at all times during work hours for the game project	1	3	1
GP2.1.0	Core	System	**FE menu system** including game title, launching of game world, player settings/options, and displaying of game credits	1	2	2
GP2.2.0	Core	Gameplay	**Game music/sound effects** for every background, collision, weapon, and character	1	2	2
GP2.3.0	Add-on	Gameplay	**Character/background selection screen** supporting every playable character and playable background	1	2	2
GP2.4.0	Add-on	Gameplay	**Robotic character theme** relating to all characters in game and storyline	1	3	2
GP2.5.0	Core	Gameplay	**Health bars/special meter bars** for each character involved in combat	1	3	2
GP2.6.0	Core	Gameplay	**Game timer** counts down during each round with the character with the most health winning when timer reaches zero	1	3	2
GP2.7.0	Add-on	Gameplay	**Safe period** of time when a round first starts where no movement or combat can occur	1	3	2
GP2.8.0	Add-on	Gameplay	**Only two robots fighting per round** in the game world with characters playing the best of three rounds	1	3	2
GP2.9.0	Add-on	Gameplay	**Side-scrolling** combat system using 3D character robots	1	3	2
GP3.1.0	Add-on	Gameplay	**Lighting/shading effects** utilized in background and foreground during gameplay	2	2	3
GP3.2.0	Core	System	**Combo system** for physical, weapon, and special move attacks	2	2	3
GP3.3.0	Core	Gameplay	**Backstory of game** explaining purpose of combat and the involvement of each robot character in the plot	2	3	3
GP3.4.0	Add-on	Gameplay	**Environmental effects** including moving background items, intractable background, and visually appealing environment	3	2	3
GP3.5.0	Add-on	System	**Achievements system** awarding bonuses for remaining health, remaining time on clock after a win, and max combo score	3	2	3
GP3.6.0	Add-on	Gameplay	**Visual damage** to attacked characters when inflicted	3	2	3

The Features List above has more detail than normal. The explanations that are next to the bolded features are not necessary; however, for those reading this that are new to the game industry, it is good practice to explain.

1. **Code** – Unique Identifier assigned to each feature

2. **Type**
   a. Core – Fundamental feature specific to genre, theme, and fun factor, built from the game design
   b. Add-on – Extra feature that adds flair and pizzazz to the game

3. **Category**
   a. Gameplay – Features that directly impact the player
   b. Tools – Production tools used to develop feature content
   c. System – Systems developed to support feature content
   d. Process – Processes that allow for successful development of the game

4. **Feature** – All important aspects of this game feature

5. **Priority** – Importance of this feature to the game, decided by producer

6. **Difficulty** – Difficulty of developing and/or creating this feature, decided by team

7. **Milestone** – A calculation combining priority and difficulty; this calculation comes with the understanding that front-loading the schedule with the hardest and most time-consuming features is always the rule

Master Task List: Game Tasks

The master task list is a list of tasks that correspond to the feature list. In that list, the features that will have tasks associated with them are the gameplay and system features. The master task list gives the producer the opportunity to have a snapshot view of what it will take to develop the game; this initial view will aid in making the production schedule, allocating resources, and refining what the game truly is or will be.

Mech Battle - War of the Future

Strategy/RPG

Master Task List

10   Hours Per Work Day

Code	Task	Priority	Estimated Hours	Actual Hours	Duration (Days)	Actual Duration	Dependencies	Risk	Resource	Milestone
G.C.1.0	Units can be organized into squads	1	120	0	12	0		High		1
G.C.1.1	Develop squad system	1	60		6	0			Nick	1
G.C.1.2	Develop squad menu interface	1	60		6	0			Preston	1
G.C.2.0	Squads can be arranged into formations	1	150	0	15	0		High		1
G.C.2.1	Develop squad formation system	1	75		7.5	0			Jeff	1
G.C.2.2	Develop squad formation menu interface	1	75		7.5	0			Colman	1
G.C.3.0	Units can acquire different spacecrafts or equipment	1	95.5	0	9.55	0		High		1
G.C.3.1	Develop base unit leveling system	1	30.5		3.05	0			Preston	1
G.C.3.2	Develop unit equipment system	1	65		6.5	0			Jimmy	1
G.C.14.0	Character attack animations	1	150.5	0	15.05	0		Medium		1
G.C.14.1	Design character attacks	1	90.5		9.05	0			Charly	1
G.C.14.2	Develop character attack animation system	1	60		6	0	Pd.C.8.0		Jimmy	1
Pd.C.8.0	Develop 3D animation system	1	60.5	0	6.05	0		Medium		1
Pd.C.8.1	Develop Maya to XNA exporter	1	30.5		3.05	0			Nick	1
Pd.C.8.2	Create generic 3D animation system	1	30		3	0			Colman	1
Pd.C.1.0	Develop level editor for spaSce-based battlefields	1	180	0	18	0		High		2
Pd.C.1.1	Implement object placement system	1	90		9	0			Jeff	2
Pd.C.1.2	Implement scripting system	1	90		9	0			Colman	2
Pd.C.3.0	Develop enemy AI squad formation system	1	160	0	16	0		Low		2
Pd.C.3.1	Determine algorithms for calculating strategic squad formations	1	70		7	0			Jimmy	2
Pd.C.3.2	Implement AI that picks strategic formations	1	90		9	0			Jimmy	2

- **Code** – Unique identifier for each feature

- **Task** – Derived from features; details work required to build features

- **Priority** – Importance to the game, decided by producer

- **Estimated Hours** – Estimated hours submitted by resources, verified by leads

- **Actual Hours** – Actual hours that the team members worked

- **Estimated Duration** – Day calculation for length of task, equal to estimated hours divided by hours per workday

- **Actual Duration** – Day calculation for length of task, equal to actual hours worked divided by hours per workday

- **Dependencies** – Any dependent tasks related to the feature

- **Risk** – Risk level for this feature

- **Resource** – Person assigned to the task

- **Milestone** – Milestone that the feature/task should start in

Capacity Plan: Resource Management

Resource management is not only managed at a relationship level, but also for the production schedule as a whole. The resources are the drivers of production while the produced items are the guidance or steering system. The capacity plan provides the producer with the available work hours for all resources on the team, making it the foundation of the production schedule. A key point of reference about capacity is that it can only increase if resources are added to the team, workdays are increased, and/or work hours are increased.

The capacity plan comes in two forms: weekly and monthly. First we will examine the weekly version, then the monthly version.

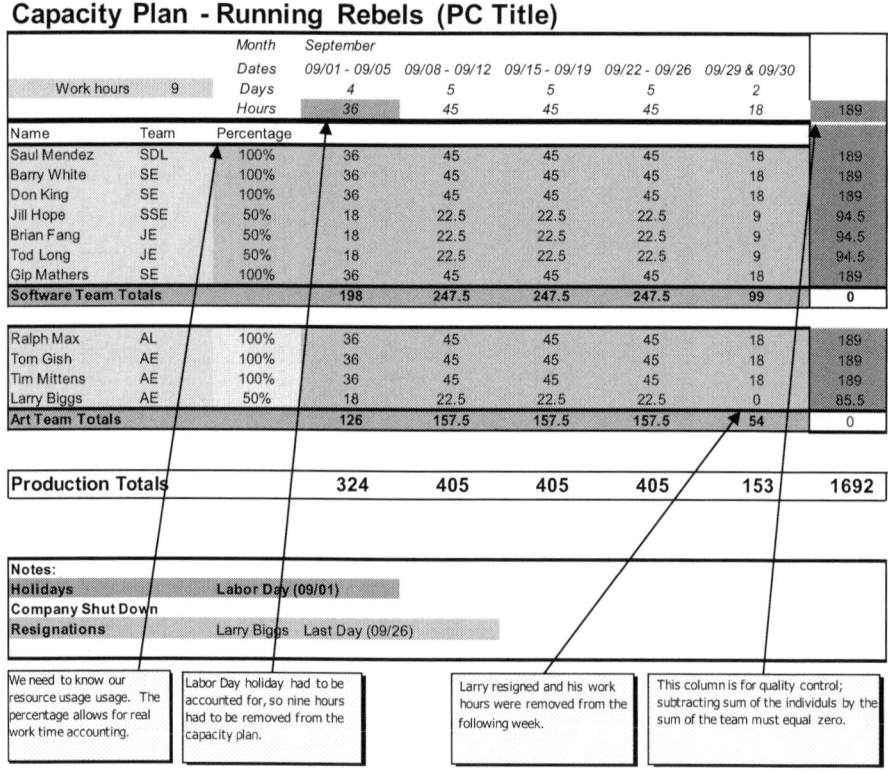

Capacity Plan - Running Rebels (PC Title)

Name	Team	Percentage	09/01 - 09/05	09/08 - 09/12	09/15 - 09/19	09/22 - 09/26	09/29 & 09/30	
		Month	September					
		Dates	09/01 - 09/05	09/08 - 09/12	09/15 - 09/19	09/22 - 09/26	09/29 & 09/30	
Work hours	9	Days	4	5	5	5	2	
		Hours	36	45	45	45	18	189
Saul Mendez	SDL	100%	36	45	45	45	18	189
Barry White	SE	100%	36	45	45	45	18	189
Don King	SE	100%	36	45	45	45	18	189
Jill Hope	SSE	50%	18	22.5	22.5	22.5	9	94.5
Brian Fang	JE	50%	18	22.5	22.5	22.5	9	94.5
Tod Long	JE	50%	18	22.5	22.5	22.5	9	94.5
Gip Mathers	SE	100%	36	45	45	45	18	189
Software Team Totals			198	247.5	247.5	247.5	99	0
Ralph Max	AL	100%	36	45	45	45	18	189
Tom Gish	AE	100%	36	45	45	45	18	189
Tim Mittens	AE	100%	36	45	45	45	18	189
Larry Biggs	AE	50%	18	22.5	22.5	22.5	0	85.5
Art Team Totals			126	157.5	157.5	157.5	54	0
Production Totals			324	405	405	405	153	1692

Notes:
Holidays   Labor Day (09/01)
Company Shut Down
Resignations   Larry Biggs   Last Day (09/26)

We need to know our resource usage usage. The percentage allows for real work time accounting.	Labor Day holiday had to be accounted for, so nine hours had to be removed from the capacity plan.	Larry resigned and his work hours were removed from the following week.	This column is for quality control; subtracting sum of the individuals by the sum of the team must equal zero.

The capacity plan displayed is the weekly capacity plan.

- **Work Hours** – Set by management and can increase if necessary

- **Name** – The team member's name

- **Team** – The level of the individual on the team

- **Percentage** – Resource percentage usage on the project, ranging from 100% (meaning the resource is fully allocated to the project) to as low as 20% (meaning the resource is part-time on the project)

- **Calculations** – Calculations are essential when building the capacity plan; by only having to monitor minimal variables, calculations allow the producer to observe and analyze situations at a glance.

- **Notes Section** – Offers clarity on issues that are unclear from just the numbers and calculations available with the capacity plan; contains information such as vacations for resources, terminations, resignations, company holidays, national holidays, and anything else that can be forecast.

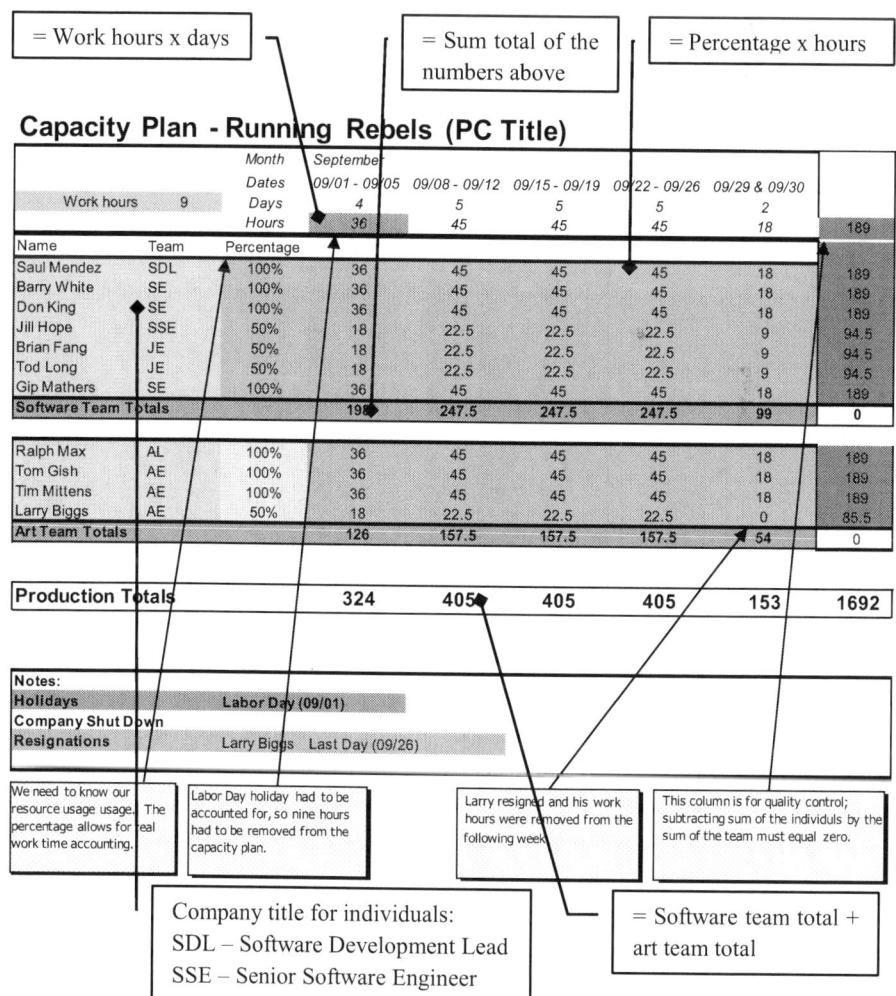

= Work hours x days

= Sum total of the numbers above

= Percentage x hours

Capacity Plan - Running Rebels (PC Title)

Name	Team	Percentage	09/01 - 09/05	09/08 - 09/12	09/15 - 09/19	09/22 - 09/26	09/29 & 09/30	
Month			September					
Dates			09/01 - 09/05	09/08 - 09/12	09/15 - 09/19	09/22 - 09/26	09/29 & 09/30	
Days			4	5	5	5	2	
Work hours 9 → Hours			36	45	45	45	18	189
Saul Mendez	SDL	100%	36	45	45	45	18	189
Barry White	SE	100%	36	45	45	45	18	189
Don King	SE	100%	36	45	45	45	18	189
Jill Hope	SSE	50%	18	22.5	22.5	22.5	9	94.5
Brian Fang	JE	50%	18	22.5	22.5	22.5	9	94.5
Tod Long	JE	50%	18	22.5	22.5	22.5	9	94.5
Gip Mathers	SE	100%	36	45	45	45	18	189
Software Team Totals			198	247.5	247.5	247.5	99	0
Ralph Max	AL	100%	36	45	45	45	18	189
Tom Gish	AE	100%	36	45	45	45	18	189
Tim Mittens	AE	100%	36	45	45	45	18	189
Larry Biggs	AE	50%	18	22.5	22.5	22.5	0	85.5
Art Team Totals			126	157.5	157.5	157.5	54	0
Production Totals			324	405	405	405	153	1692

Notes:
Holidays   Labor Day (09/01)
Company Shut Down
Resignations   Larry Biggs   Last Day (09/26)

> We need to know our resource usage usage. The percentage allows for real work time accounting.

> Labor Day holiday had to be accounted for, so nine hours had to be removed from the capacity plan.

> Larry resigned and his work hours were removed from the following week

> This column is for quality control; subtracting sum of the individuls by the sum of the team must equal zero.

Company title for individuals:
SDL – Software Development Lead
SSE – Senior Software Engineer

= Software team total + art team total

Next is the monthly form of the capacity plan, which you can see below. The monthly capacity plan would be considered the macro level of game resource management.

Biltz Buzz

Monthly Capacity Plan - Year 2011

		Month:	January	February	March	April	May	June	
Hours:	**10**	**Days:**	20	19	23	21	21	22	
		Hours:	200	190	230	210	210	220	
	Names	**Percentage**							
Development Team	James Parker	100%	200	190	230	210	210	220	
	Stan Quash	100%	200	190	230	210	210	220	
	Anthony Williams	100%	200	190	230	210	210	220	
	Justin Cannady	50%	100	95	115	105	105	110	
	Dev Team Totals:		**700**	**665**	**805**	**735**	**735**	**770**	
Art Team	Lidia Wills	100%	200	190	230	210	210	220	
	Paul White-Davis	100%	200	190	230	210	210	220	
	Shereen Morris	100%	200	190	230	210	210	220	
	Lisa Holt	50%	100	95	115	105	105	110	
	Art Team Totals:		**700**	**665**	**805**	**735**	**735**	**770**	
	Production Totals:		**1400**	**1330**	**1610**	**1470**	**1470**	**1540**	**8820**

Notes	
2011 National Holidays:	January 1st, Saturday, New Year's Day
	January 17th, Monday, Martin Luther King Jr.'s Birthday
	February 21st, Monday, Washington's Birthday
	May 30th, Monday, Memorial Day

The capacity plan displayed is the monthly capacity plan.

- **Names** – The team members' names

- **Calculations** – Calculations are essential when building the Capacity Plan; by only having to monitor minimal variables, the producer is able to observe and analyze situations at a glance.

- **Notes Section** – Offers clarity on issues that are unclear from just the numbers and calculations available with the capacity plan; contains information such as vacations for resources, terminations, resignations, company holidays, national holidays, and anything else that can be forecast.

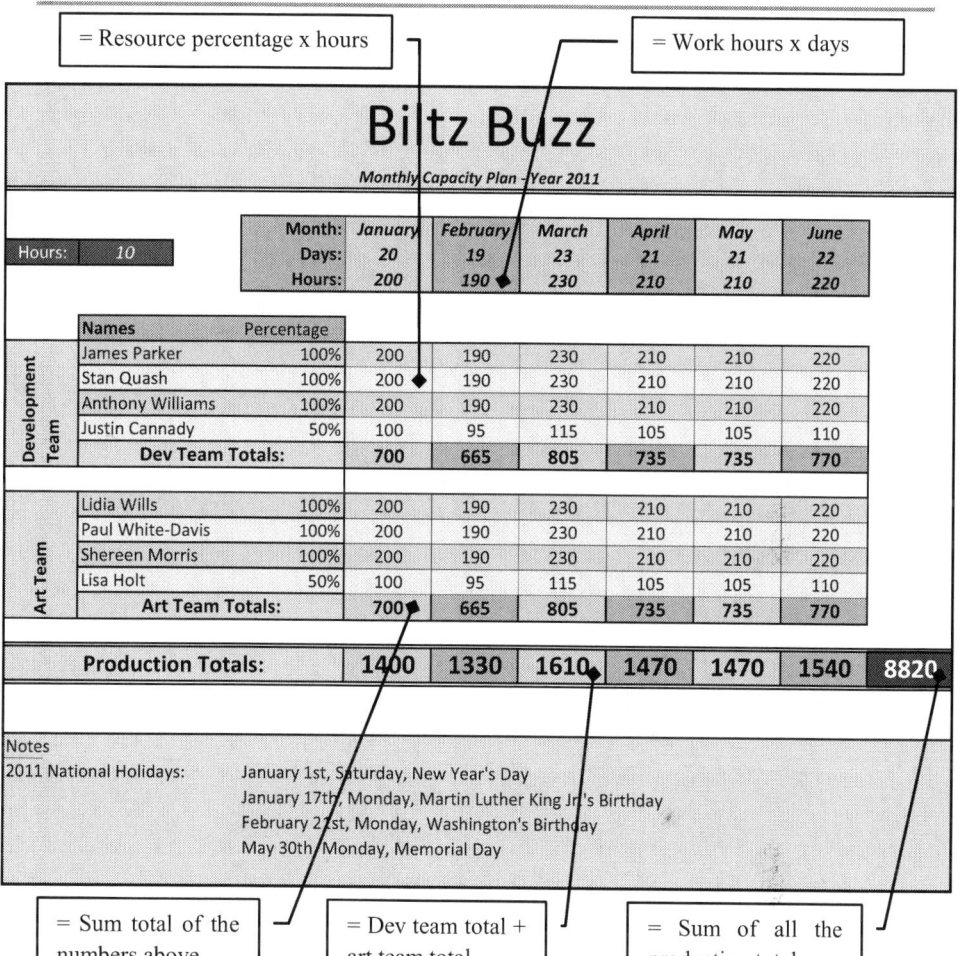

= Resource percentage x hours

= Work hours x days

Blitz Buzz

Monthly Capacity Plan - Year 2011

		Month:	January	February	March	April	May	June
Hours:	**10**	Days:	20	19	23	21	21	22
		Hours:	200	190	230	210	210	220

	Names	Percentage						
Development Team	James Parker	100%	200	190	230	210	210	220
	Stan Quash	100%	200	190	230	210	210	220
	Anthony Williams	100%	200	190	230	210	210	220
	Justin Cannady	50%	100	95	115	105	105	110
	Dev Team Totals:		**700**	**665**	**805**	**735**	**735**	**770**
Art Team	Lidia Wills	100%	200	190	230	210	210	220
	Paul White-Davis	100%	200	190	230	210	210	220
	Shereen Morris	100%	200	190	230	210	210	220
	Lisa Holt	50%	100	95	115	105	105	110
	Art Team Totals:		**700**	**665**	**805**	**735**	**735**	**770**
Production Totals:			**1400**	**1330**	**1610**	**1470**	**1470**	**1540**	**8820**

Notes
2011 National Holidays: January 1st, Saturday, New Year's Day
January 17th, Monday, Martin Luther King Jr's Birthday
February 21st, Monday, Washington's Birthday
May 30th, Monday, Memorial Day

= Sum total of the numbers above

= Dev team total + art team total

= Sum of all the production totals

Managing the Capacity Plan

The only ways to increase the capacity within a game project are:

- Increasing assigned work hours
- Increasing allowed work days
- Adding resources to the team
- Increasing usage percentage (if possible) of people lower than 100%

Please note there are only twenty-four hours in a day and only seven days in a week, and those variables have maximum levels that cannot be exceeded. Adding more people to the game production phase is the most common solution to this problem, but depending on the studio size, increasing the size of the game production team can be a net positive or a net negative.

Cut List: Features/Tasks That Are Removed

The cut list provides a place for features and tasks that for one reason or another get removed from the production schedule. Several factors – like realignment of priorities, resources, and/or tasks – may cause the list to expand; however, just because features and tasks make it to the cut list doesn't mean that the list is their final fate. As production moves forward, the same realignment of priorities, resources, and/or tasks can take those elements exiled to the cut list and return them to the production schedule.

CUT LIST

Code	Task Description	Estimate	Dependencies	Risk	Resources	Milestone
G.E.4.0	24 hour Environment	500	G.C.2.0	High		3
G.E.4.0.1	Code Environment Changes	300		High	Brian	3
G.E.4.0.2	Code Optimization	100		Med	Chris	3
G.E.4.0.3	Implementation	100		Med	Dan	3

G.E.4.0.1
G.E.4.0.2
G.E.4.0.3 - Are the tasks needing to be completed for FEATURE G.E.4.0 to be considered done.

G.E.4.0 - Actual feature from feature List

Indicates the milestone that the feature and tasks are being cut from.

- **Code** – Unique identifier from feature list

- **Task Description** – Feature description derived from feature list

- **Estimate** – Hours from production schedule

- **Dependencies** – All dependent tasks related to the feature

- **Risk** –Risk level from master task list

- **Resources** – Person(s) assigned to the task

- **Milestone** – Milestone that feature was removed from

Cut Process for the Producer

Prior to the actual Cut Session – the meeting where the producer/production leader presents the information and reasoning for making a feature cut – the producer/production leader has to consider the following:

- **Core Features** – Realizing what the game truly is, e.g., a car-racing game cutting the cars would be ludicrous.

- **Prioritization** – Higher-priority features/tasks should not be cut, due to the fact they are core features and/or core-supporting.

- **Time** – All schedules are based on time. Once in production, time becomes a factor that can make or break a game. Being aware of where the project is currently and how much time is remaining is crucial to the success of production.

- **Dependency** – Features/tasks are sometimes connected by how the game is built. This also must be taken into account when making the cut decision.

- **Resource** – Making cuts directly affects how work is done by the resources. When rescheduling the overall project, the producer must take into account the resources' skill sets.

Cut Session

The Cut Session is a meeting that can be very uncomfortable. Some team members may feel personally connected to a feature or task, and may take it personally when that feature or task is removed. Thus it is imperative that the producer/production leader stress that all decisions made are what is best for the game. In this meeting transparency is critical, and three items need to be discussed:

- **Review of All Features** – Discussing all cut features and their impact on the game

- **Resource Allocation** – Making the team aware of their reallocation

- **Time/Schedule** – Transparently outlining the new/adjusted game production schedule

Quality Test List: Game Quality Verification

The quality test list is a representation of the overall test list (a long, detailed document correlated to the feature list that contains every possible test for the game). A key part of this list are requirements; that is, the functionality of said features. A producer needs to fully understand how these features are going to work in-game so he or she can write out the proper requirements, and this can be done with the technical and art leads that are assigned to the team. A producer must also remember to update the quality test plan list throughout production since features may be moved from one milestone to another, cut, or modified due to time constraints, technology development, or other such issues.

Red Hat Detective					
Game Test Plan List					
Milestone	Code	Description	Requirements	Pass/Fail	Comments
1	GP.07.00	In-game dossiers on persons of interest	-	FAIL	
			Dossier screen displays correct information	Pass	
			Player can select which person's dossier to read	Pass	
			Dossiers only show information compiled so far	Pass	
			Dossier information scrolls properly	Pass	
			Player can exit dossier screen successfully	Fail	Upon exit, dossier background graphic remains overlaid on screen. (Tested at beginning of Case 1; confirmed using midpoint save of Case 3) 06/16/10 12:08p Jordan Merritt
1	GP.08.00	Primary rifle	-	PASS	
			Primary rifle fired	Pass	
			Primary rifle stops firing	Pass	
			Primary rifle fires 3round burst	Pass	
2	GP.14.00	HUD	-	PASS	
			HUD displays correctly in-game	Pass	
			HUD displays statistics correctly	Pass	
			HUD updates information correctly, as appropriate	Pass	
			HUD disappears when appropriate	Pass	
2	GP.23.00	Location: Nick Peril's Office	-	FAIL	
			Location displays correctly	Pass	
			Location and objects have correct solidity	Fail	Can walk through couch on south wall. 06/16/10 1:14p Isaiah Harris
			Can initiate save menu from file cabinet	Pass	
			Can initiate load menu from file cabinet	Pass	
			Can initiate dossiers screen from desk	Pass	
3	GP.32.00	Clue-gathering system (both psychic and mundane)	-	FAIL	
			Clues are 'picked up' appropriate to script	Pass	
			Clues from dialogue are logged	Pass	
			Clues from surface thoughts are logged	Pass	
			Clues from objects are logged	Pass	
			Gathered clues allow progression through story	Fail	Gathered enough clues to progress to final reveal in Case 2 (according to script) but was unable to progress. 06/16/10 1:43p Jordan Merritt
3	GP.06.00	Collapsible building	-	PASS	
			Building must collapse	Pass	
			Building pieces must collide properly	Pass	
			Building must display in game	Pass	
4	GP.31.00	Closing cutscene	-	PASS	
			Cutscene displays following end of game	Pass	
			Cutscene sound, visuals are synched	Pass	
			Cutscene displays with proper framerate	Pass	
			Cutscene provides impressive visuals	Pass	
			Cutscene ends, brings up opening menu properly	Pass	
5	GP.17.00	On-screen mini-map	-	FAIL	
			Mini-map displays correctly	Pass	
			Mini-map shows location of player correctly	Fail	Mini-map icon stuck at entrance location; does not track with player movements. 06/16/10 2:05p Jade Blake
			Mini-map shows location of NPCs correctly	Pass	

- **Milestone** – The milestone that the feature can be tested in

- **Code** – Unique identifier from feature list
- **Description** – Feature description derived from feature list

- **Requirements** – Tests that have to pass within gameplay for the feature to be verified

- **Pass/Fail** – Simple pass/fail section for producer to maintain until all game requirements successfully pass

- **Comments** – Section for producer to take notes on fails, which will turn into bug reports

Risk List: Factors That May Jeopardize Game Production

The risk list provides the producer/production leader with all the risks that can negatively impact the game production and schedule, and the producer/production leader should always be mindful and aware of these risks. Risks can be associated with people or tasks, ranging in impact from minimal to game-halting, and these risks should all have a single mitigating solution, so there is no confusion in which direction the game production will go if these risks are realized.

RISK LIST						
Description	Probability of Occurring	Impact on Project	Risk Classification	Decision Date	Resource	Mitigation Strategies
GP 07.8 - 24-hour Environmental Change	High	Med	Med	2/11/2022	Gwin	Static environments throughout the game
Luis has been out for 1 week (SICK)	High	High	High	3/2/2022	Luis	Make cutsto game to address loss of resource
GP 09.3 - Laser Locking Pistol	Low	Med	Med	4/5/2022	Jefferson	Regular pistol

- **Description** – The risk that may hinder the project

- **Probability of Occurring** – The probability of the risk being realized

- **Impact on Project** – Potential impact on the game production schedule

- **Risk Classification** – Overall risk value on the production schedule

- **Decision Date** –The date that the mitigation strategy will be enacted

- **Resource** – The person assigned to the task

- **Mitigation Strategies** – Solution for the risk

Risks in game production are not only game-related - such as feature creep, hardware, or even pipeline interruptions - but also people-related; i.e., having to do with resources. Resources are a production's greatest asset, but also the greatest risk. Because video games are not developed by machines, which would mean the producer/production leader would work in a controlled environment, there is always a risk involved with people. Having resources on the project adds a layer of complexity when dealing with egos, pride, outside issues, etc. A successful producer/production leader manages the people along with the production; if the people on the game project are managed effectively and efficiently, then production becomes more manageable, with obstacles being proactively resolved.

Game Production Schedule: AKA "The Road Map"

The game production schedule is a document that is a marriage of the capacity plan, master task list, and in the mid-to-late iterations of it, the cut list as well. Once the constraints of the capacity are known, it is up to the producer/production leader to decide what tasks from the master task list will get scheduled to make up the game production schedule.

The Gantt chart formatting of this document is important to the success of the production phase of the game development life cycle. Documentation needs to be able to support itself, in the sense that, if the producer is not readily available for whatever reason, then anyone should be able to pick up the Gantt chart and follow the work that has been occurring on the project's workflow.

In this section the focus will be on the items that have the highest impact on game production. The snapshots below show one of many ways to build the Gantt chart. Below, you can see how information from the capacity plan and master task list is merged together to build the production schedule.

When building the project file, it is important to setup your base calendar first:

Note: When MS Project is open, Tools, Options, and Calendars allow the user to set up the base calendar the way it needs to be for the production schedule they are managing.

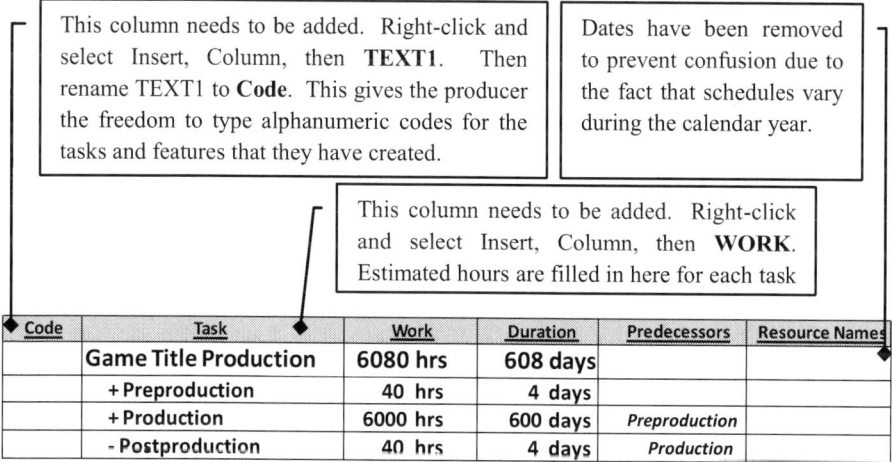

This column needs to be added. Right-click and select Insert, Column, then **TEXT1**. Then rename TEXT1 to **Code**. This gives the producer the freedom to type alphanumeric codes for the tasks and features that they have created.

Dates have been removed to prevent confusion due to the fact that schedules vary during the calendar year.

This column needs to be added. Right-click and select Insert, Column, then **WORK**. Estimated hours are filled in here for each task

Code	Task	Work	Duration	Predecessors	Resource Names
	Game Title Production	**6080 hrs**	**608 days**		
	+ Preproduction	40 hrs	4 days		
	+ Production	6000 hrs	600 days	*Preproduction*	
	- Postproduction	40 hrs	4 days	*Production*	

Note: This production schedule is based off a ten (10) hour workday, five (5) workdays in a week.

Code	Task	Work	Duration	Predecessors	Resource Names
	Game Title Production	**6080 hrs**	**608 days**		
	- Preproduction	40 hrs	4 days		
	Feature List	5 hrs	0.5 days		*Producer*
	Master Task List	10 hrs	1 days	*Feature List*	*Producer*
	Capacity Plan	5 hrs	0.5 days		*Producer*
	Production Schedule	20 hrs	2 days	*Master Task List & Capacity Plan*	*Producer*
	+ Production	6000 hrs	600 days	*Preproduction*	
	+ Postproduction	40 hrs	4 days	*Production*	

Notice that the three phases of the game development life cycle (page 9 for more detail) are all prominent in the production schedule. By making the three phases prominent, the producer is able to see a global perspective of the time required to complete the game.

> The Production total should match the capacity plan's overall total of team hours. Each milestone total should match with each monthly team capacity total.

Code	Task	Work	Duration	Predecessors	Resource Names
	Game Title Production	**6080 hrs**	**608 days**		
	+ Preproduction	40 hrs	4 days		
	- Production	6000 hrs ◆	600 days	*Preproduction*	
	- Milestone One	750 hrs	75 days		
	+ Dev Tasks	290 hrs	29 days		
	+ Art Tasks	290 hrs	29 days		
	+ Quality	75 hrs	7 days		
	+ Contigency	75 hrs	7 days		
	+ Meetings	20 hrs	2 days		
	+ Milestone Two	900 hrs	90 days	*Milestone One*	
	+ Milestone Three	1100 hrs	110 days	*Milestone Two*	
	+ Milestone Four	1250 hrs	125 days	*Milestone Three*	
	+ Milestone Five	1200 hrs	120 days	*Milestone Four*	
	+ Milestone Six	800 hrs	80 days	*Milestone Five*	
	+ Postproduction	40 hrs	4 days	*Production*	

The production phase is a key section to focus on, as this is where the milestones are designated and planned out. A producer/production leader needs to make sure when building the game production schedule that the hours correlate to the capacity plan.

Milestone One's sub-tasks represent all the planned activities that go into the development of the game, which include:

- Development Tasks
- Art Tasks
- Quality Assurance
- Contingency Planning
- Meetings

Code	Task	Work	Duration	Predecessors	Resource Names
	Game Title Production	6080 hrs	608 days		
	+ Preproduction	40 hrs	4 days		
	- Production	6000 hrs	600 days	Preproduction	
	- Milestone One	750 hrs	75 days		
	+ Dev Tasks	290 hrs	29 days		
	+ Art Tasks	290 hrs	29 days		
	+ Quality	75 hrs	7 days		
	+ Contigency	75 hrs	7 days		
	+ Meetings	20 hrs	2 days		
	+ Milestone Two	900 hrs	90 days	Milestone One	
	+ Milestone Three	1100 hrs	110 days	Milestone Two	
	+ Milestone Four	1250 hrs	125 days	Milestone Three	
	+ Milestone Five	1200 hrs	120 days	Milestone Four	
	+ Milestone Six	800 hrs	80 days	Milestone Five	
	+ Postproduction	40 hrs	4 days	Production	

Unique identifier established in the beginning of the project by the producer.

Notice the feature is also in the schedule with its corresponding tasks(s).

Code	Task	Work	Duration	Predecessors	Resource Names
	- Milestone One	1500 hrs	150 days		
	- Dev Tasks	600 hrs	60 days		
PD03	-XNA for basic game engine	250 hrs	25 days		
PD03A	Research Engine (p1)	250 hrs	25 days		Debbie Jordan
GP30	-Campaign Mode	125 hrs	12.5 days		
GP30A	Design (p1)	125 hrs	12.5 days		James Parker
PD01	-Collision system	115 hrs	11.5 days		
PD01A	Design (p1)	115 hrs	11.5 days		Brandy Marsh
PD02	-Physics system	110 hrs	11 days		
PD02A	Design (p1)	110 hrs	11 days		Stanley Quash

Tasks can be completed across multiple milestones. The code stays the same for each item.

Resources are assigned to the task level, not the feature.

Quality assurance and contingency planning are both ten (10) percent of a resource's original capacity. Example: if Senior Programmer Stanley Quash's milestone two capacity is 300 hours, then his quality assurance time is 30 hours and his contingency time is also 30 hours.

The meeting time is a grey area, which depends on the producer/production leader's discretion as to how many meetings their team should have and how long. Normally you will see planning meetings, mid-week review meetings, and end-week review meetings (these meetings usually last an hour each):

- **Planning** – Resource assignments and setting of expectations

- **Mid-week Review** – Discussions on progress, any possible changes in the schedule, and any issues with features or tasks

- **End-week Review** – Accomplishments and any cuts for the week, and any last-minute changes to the schedule

Code	Task	Work	Duration	Predecessors	Resource Names
	- Milestone One	1200 hrs	120 days		
	+ Dev Tasks	600 hrs	60 days		
	- Art Tasks	474 hrs	47.4 days		
	- Quality	60 hrs	6 days		
	Stanley Quash	60 hrs	6 days		Stanley Quash
	- Contingency	30 hrs	3 days		
	Debbie Jordan	30 hrs	3 days		Debbie Jordan
	- Meetings	36 hrs	3.6 days		
	Planning Sessions	12 hrs	1.2 days		Team
	Mid-week Reviews	12 hrs	1.2 days		Team
	End-week Reviews & Cut Sessions	12 hrs	1.2 days		Team

Code	Task	Work	Duration	Predecessors	Resource Names
	Game Title Production	**6080 hrs**	**608 days**		
	+ Preproduction	40 hrs	4 days		
	+ Production	6000 hrs	600 days	Preproduction	
	+ Postproduction	40 hrs	4 days	Production	
	Gold Master	750 hrs	75 days		Producer
	Game Archiving	290 hrs	29 days		Producer
	Game Post-mortem	290 hrs	29 days		Producer

Postproduction is different for each studio. What is shown above are the basic tasks that can be performed in this phase. It can be expanded to capture more detail if necessary.

Game Production: Know What You Have To Manage

Since video games are a visual medium, producers/production leaders need to understand the idea of what deliverables are and what their expected impact on the game will be. Game content goes through several phases prior to being considered "in" the game:

- **Milestone** – A period of development time, specified as complete with some form of criteria or deliverable

- **Deliverables** – Uploaded, played, or displayed

A solid deliverable starts as a game feature that is "uploaded" onto the server; then, after being compiled, the game feature needs to be "played" in-game. Finally, the game feature needs to be "displayed", which refers to not only visual components, but also other sensory elements such as audio features and controller vibration.

- **Uploaded** – Code and/or art has been developed and added to the folder structure of the game

- **Played** – Code and/or art is operating in the game

- **Displayed** – The final phase where feedback - i.e. visualization - has occurred and the player is actually playing the feature in-game

Production Schedule: Master Task List and Capacity Plan

The production schedule is built from the team's capacity and the prioritized tasks from the master task list. The producer/production leader needs to understand that the team is limited by their overall capacity (please see page 26 for capacity plan understanding). It is critical that numbers correlate across from the capacity plan to the production schedule. Two key points that a producer/production leader should remember:

- Tasks can span across multiple milestones
- Individual tasks should only have one resource, for proper workflow tracking

Remember, a fine balance between production and game fixes is essential to the success of the game development lifecycle. Here are some good sample divisions:

- **3/1 Work Month** – Three weeks of game production and one week of quality assurance

- **3/2 Work Week** – Three days of game production and two days of quality assurance

- **6/2 Workday** – Six hours of game production and two hours of quality assurance

Communication Is Key

For a producer/production leader, communication should always be flowing three ways: upwards to executives and superiors, downwards to team leads and members, and horizontally to other producers and peers.

Managing Up – Keeping Your Boss in the Know

Being a producer/production leader is a difficult role. It requires discipline, balance, proactive thinking, intelligent problem solving, people skills, and creativity. One aspect of this position that some people overlook is maintaining communication upwards: "keeping your boss in the know." What does that mean? It means your immediate superior, who could be an executive producer, senior producer, development manager, etc., should never be without a timely update on the project. Now "timely" may sound subjective, but it is not; weekly project statuses should be sent without request to superiors, containing key/critical information in a bulleted format (no fluff), including, but not limited to, the following:

- Key Accomplishments
- Star Resources
- Cuts
- Critical Issues (resource-level up to project-based)
- High Risks (top five)
- Build Number (if applicable)
- Overall Project Status (on-budget/on-schedule, etc.)
- Needs (things that would make managing the project easier)

Most importantly, this should all fit on <u>one page</u>, so figure out a good format. The benefit of keeping your superior in the know is that it allows you to manage the project better. Your superior will be more likely to address your project's needs, discuss and resolve issues, and avoid negatively influencing the team.

On the following page is an AOI template you can use for presenting information to your boss:

Game Team	Game Title	
Weekly Status Report	**Week of**	
Accomplishments	This section has the previous week's completed work objectives.	
Objectives	This section contains tasks and/or any work planned for the current week.	
Issues	This section has any issues that are currently present in the project.	

1. **Accomplishments, Objectives and Issues** – AOI Template provided above

2. **One-on-One** – Direct meetings scheduled with executives/superiors
   - Status Reports – Weekly updates consist of high risks that can derail production
   - Milestone deliverables
   - Bugs addressed
   - Bright stars – team members who have performed beyond the normal day to day tasks

Downward Communication – Team Leads and Members

1. **Newsletters** – Discuss the progress of the game, as team members are often surprisingly unaware of how the overall game is shaping up. Sometimes they are so immersed in their tasks that they miss the big picture.

2. **Meeting Minutes** – Should be provided in a timely fashion to the whole team, and resources should also be assigned to each action item. Also, all action items need due dates that leads should follow up with regularly.

3. **Team Meetings** – Should be scheduled with agendas provided to the entire team prior to starting. The meetings should be conducted in an orderly fashion, allowing the producer/production leader to speak and complete the agenda prior to dealing with any questions the team has. Proper attendance should be addressed from the start, and minimizing any distractions (e.g., tardy people, cell phones, etc.) is essential.

Horizontal Communication - Producers

Group Meetings – The group meetings are where producers/production leaders can discuss issues with one another, find ways to make improvements to production, deal with conflicts, and discuss exciting new ideas.

Bugs & Quality Philosophy: Not Just Testing and Fixing

Quality Philosophy

It is critical to the overall success of the game that a "quality philosophy" is established in preproduction. What does this mean? Simple: the producer/production leader cannot just wait for the quality department to do all the quality assurance testing. The producer/production leader is just as familiar with the game mechanics, story, and design aspects as the QA department. Instilling a quality focus in all the members on the team will be the common thread all the way through production. The idea of dealing with the "bugs" upfront is not truly new, but the idea of solving each "bug" as it comes up *is* new.

This philosophy will aid in producing games with little to no "bugs" at all. This may seem impossible, but not if you remember this is software (code) to be wrapped with art (graphics), and thus is similar to the software application programs of today that have to abide by strict standards such as Capability Maturity Model Integration (CMMI) by the Software Engineering Institute (SEI).

Team Quality Management (TQM)

The concept of team quality management means allowing the team to become self-governing when it comes to the "bugs". It is a process of team building, bug solving, and member development. The critics of this ideology would say that it takes too much time away from production, that it can become a distraction, and that it directly causes feature creep. I will agree that it will slow down production on the front end; however, as production progresses, the speed of development will increase due to the maturing of associate- and mid-level developers and artists.

Asset Management Overview

Game assets are everything that is in the game, which includes:

- Game audio
- Cutscenes
- Game art
- Code

These assets have to be properly managed throughout the entire production. The asset count can be extraordinarily high, and maintaining accurate accounting of those assets can be quite arduous. It is vital that the producer/production leader understands all the important properties of these assets, including:

- Asset Risk
- Asset Control
- Naming Convention
- Server Location
- Game Version Control

Asset Risk
- Can be modified by more than one person
- Can change over time
- Can be misplaced or incorrectly named

Asset Control
- Having an asset management system to aid in the control process of all game assets is essential. There are many kinds of asset management systems that allow a producer/production leader to manage how an asset is processed. These systems can be configured to have all new or modified assets reviewed and approved prior to uploading to the server, and email notifications can also be added to enhance accountability. Finally, asset management systems can give an historical record of asset development throughout game production.

Naming Convention
- Defining the naming convention in preproduction is crucial for the success of production. The naming convention needs to be known to the whole team so that game assets are identified properly.

Server Location

- In preproduction, establishing a location for all game content and game documentation is important for the management of production and postproduction.

Game Version Control

- Managing game builds is another aspect of the production phase. Game builds are a form of progression verification, because game quality includes not only game content, but also game design and how enjoyable the game is to play.

Rules of Game Production

1. Never abandon your plans

2. All production documentation will become your production roadmap

3. Unforeseen situations will always occur; be flexible

4. All decisions made should be directed towards improving game quality

5. People are your number one risk

6. Implementing a quality philosophy on the front end of production will improve overall game quality

7. Never delete any of your documents; always "save as"

8. Utilize past performance metrics as estimate guides for future milestones

9. Build some freedom into your schedule

10. Understand that not all features designed in the beginning will get into the game

11. Conduct, at minimum, a twice-a-week status assessment

12. Testing is an integral part of game quality

13. Provide weekly status reports to game project executives and superiors

14. Communicate all aspects of milestone reviews to all parties

15. For each milestone, deliver a detailed description of the milestone features and corresponding tasks

16. For each milestone, set up project tracking metrics, including updated/correct numbers, bug details, times/dates, and distribution lists

17. Establish a plan as to when / how game builds will be produced (i.e. daily, biweekly, monthly, etc.)

18. Keep stakeholders informed throughout production

19. Have solutions for issues prior to presenting those issues to your supervisor

Made in the USA
Coppell, TX
15 October 2021